For the veterans
—J.B.

To Jen, whose words make pictures in my mind
—M.S.

THIS IS A BORZOI BOOK PUBLISHED BY ALFRED A. KNOPF • Text copyright © 2013 by Jennifer Bryant • Jacket art and interior illustrations copyright © 2013 by Melissa Sweet • All rights reserved. Published in the United States by Alfred A. Knopf, an imprint of Random House Children's Books, a division of Random House, Inc., New York. Knopf, Borzoi Books, and the colophon are registered trademarks of Random House, Inc. • Visit us on the Web! randomhouse.com/kids • Educators and librarians, for a variety of teaching tools, visit us at RHTeachersLibrarians.com • *Library of Congress Cataloging-in-Publication Data* • Bryant, Jennifer. A splash of red : the life and art of Horace Pippin / by Jen Bryant ; illustrated by Melissa Sweet. — 1st ed. • p. cm. • ISBN 978-0-375-86712-5 (trade) — ISBN 978-0-375-96712-2 (lib. bdg.) • [1. Pippin, Horace, 1888–1946—Juvenile literature. 2. African American painters—Biography—Juvenile literature. 3. Painters— United States—Biography—Juvenile literature.] I. Sweet, Melissa, ill. II. Title. • ND237.P65 B79 2013 • 759.13—dc23 • [B] • 2012003209

The text of this book is set in 19-point Galena Condensed.
The illustrations were created using watercolor, gouache, and mixed media.

Image credits: Historical note: "Horace Pippin painting *Man Seated Near Stove*," photograph reprinted from *Horace Pippin: A Negro Painter in America* by Selden Rodman, copyright © 1947, 1972 by Selden Rodman, courtesy of the Estate of Selden Rodman. Back endpapers: *Self Portrait,* 1941, oil on canvas board, courtesy of Albright-Knox Art Gallery/Art Resource, Buffalo, NY; *The Bear Hunt I,* 1930, courtesy of Chester County Historical Society, West Chester, PA; *Cabin in the Cotton,* 1933–1937, oil on cotton mounted on Masonite, photograph © The Art Institute of Chicago, Chicago, IL; *The End of the War: Starting Home,* 1930–1933, oil on canvas, courtesy of Philadelphia Museum of Art, Philadelphia, PA; *Saying Prayers,* 1943, oil on canvas, courtesy of Brandywine River Museum, Chadds Ford, PA, Museum Purchase, 1980, The Betsy James Wyeth Fund.

MANUFACTURED IN CHINA • January 2013 • 10 9 8 7 6 5 • First Edition

A SPLASH OF RED

THE LIFE AND ART OF HORACE PIPPIN

written by Jen Bryant   illustrated by Melissa Sweet

ALFRED A. KNOPF 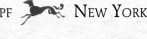 NEW YORK

On February 22, 1888, the town of West Chester, Pennsylvania, celebrated a holiday. That day, in that same town, Daniel and Christine Pippin celebrated the birth of their son, Horace.

Horace grew fast—so fast that his mother could barely
keep up with the mending. "He'll be a giant someday,"
the neighbors would say. Grandma Pippin smiled at Horace's
long legs and big hands. She figured the neighbors were right.

Grandma's hands were big, too—rough and scarred
from her slave days in Virginia. But they were just fine
for giving Horace hugs. "The biggest part of you," she told him,
"is inside, where no one can see."

When Horace was three years old, the Pippins moved
to Goshen, New York. As the family grew larger, everyone helped out.

Horace put his big hands to work. He fetched flour for his mother.
He sorted laundry with his sisters. He played with his baby brother.
He held the horse while the driver delivered milk.

At night, he piled wood for the stove and arranged
dominoes so his grandmother could play. Then,
if he could find a scrap of paper and a piece of charcoal,
he drew pictures of what he'd seen that day.

Horace loved to draw. He loved the feel of the charcoal
as it slid across the floor. He loved looking at something
in the room and making it come alive again in front of him.
He loved thinking about a friend or a pet, then drawing them
from the picture in his mind.

At school, he sat quietly at his desk, but his big hands
were always busy.
"Make a picture for us, Horace!" his classmates said.
And Horace did.

His pictures made people happy.
Except when he made some next to his spelling list. . . .
That made the teacher mad!

hen

dog stove tree

fish

star dishpan book

Pictures just come to my mind...

and I tell my heart to go ahead.

But Horace couldn't stop drawing.

One day, Horace saw a funny face in a magazine.
DRAW ME! AND WIN A PRIZE, it said underneath.
Horace drew the face and sent it off.

A few weeks later, a package arrived. Inside, Horace found colored pencils, a pair of brushes, and a box of paints.

CONGRATULATIONS! said the note.

Horace had won his first real art supplies.

"*Paint* a picture for us, Horace!" his sisters cried.

And Horace did. He painted everyday scenes in natural colors; then he added a splash of red.

Hattie and the Rooster

Horace was in eighth grade when his father left for good.
The family needed money, so Horace quit school
and went to work.

For several years, Horace's big hands were *always* busy:
stacking grain sacks at a feed store,
shoveling coal at a rail yard,
mending fences on a farm,
carrying luggage at a hotel,
making brakes in an iron factory . . .

. . . packing oil paintings into large wooden crates.
Looking at these made Horace remember winning the art contest.
How proud he'd been! How he'd loved those colored pencils,
those brushes, and his first real box of paints!

Horace was a big man now, with big responsibilities.
Still, he loved drawing as much as he always had.
He used charcoal, broken pencils, whatever he could find.
"Make a picture for us, Horace!" the other workers said.
And Horace did.

Far across the ocean, a terrible war had begun.
Horace's big heart wanted to help.

The Good old U.S.A.
was in trouble
with Germany.

He joined the army and sailed away.

In France, Horace and his regiment dug deep trenches
for protection. There were no blankets or beds. It was always
wet and cold and dark.

I have not seen the sun in more than a month.

"I have not seen the sun in more than a month,"
Horace wrote. He wrapped his big hands around a rifle.
Planes droned overhead. Shells exploded. Gunfire rattled through the night.

If the fighting stopped for a while, Horace put down his gun
and picked up a pencil. "Make a picture for us, Horace!"
his soldier friends pleaded. And Horace did. He filled his notebooks,
one by one.

THE War brought out all the Art in me

One day, he climbed to the top of the trench.
A shot rang out.
Horace felt pain in his shoulder. He was hit!

Many hours passed before help came.

Horace was glad to be alive. But the bullet
had badly damaged his right arm. When it healed,
he couldn't lift or move it the way he used to.
Now, when someone said, "Make a picture for us, Horace!" . . .
Horace could not.

After the war, Horace came back to the United States
and met Jennie Wade. Jennie was a hard worker.
She loved to cook. Horace was a hard worker, too.
And he loved to eat! It was a good match.
They married and settled down in West Chester.

HORACE & JENNIE PIPPIN

NOV. 20, 1920

I can never forget Suffering AND I will never forget SUNSET. I CAME HOME WITH ALL OF it IN MY MIND.

Horace was thirty-two years old, as big and as strong as ever.
But because of his injured arm, he couldn't find a job.
"How much can you lift?" the hiring boss asked.
And that was the end of that.

So . . . Horace did what he could. He organized a Boy Scout troop.
He umpired baseball games. He took the neighbors'
children fishing. When Jennie started a laundry business,
Horace delivered the clean clothes.

As he walked along the streets of West Chester, his fingers
itched to draw all the colors and textures he saw:
     lacy white curtains billowing in the windows,
     a splash of red geraniums blooming on a step,
     a yellow cat sprinting down an alley,
     deep green vines spiraling up a wall.

At night, his old home in Goshen, his grandmother's slave days,
and the Bible stories she'd told made pictures in his mind.
He longed to draw them, too. But how?
His right arm was weak and painful to lift.

The iron poker stood by the fire, straight and tall as a soldier.
Could he . . . ?

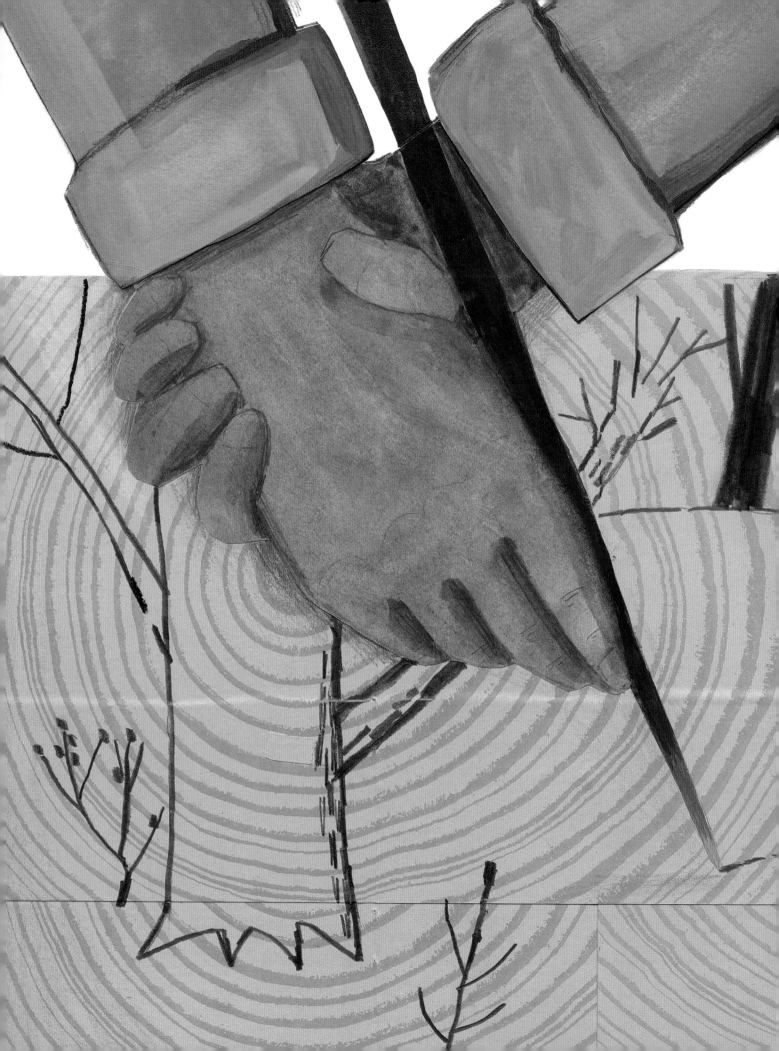

With his left hand, he grasped his right wrist. He thrust the poker
into the flames until it glowed red-hot. Using his good arm
to move the hurt one, he scorched lines into wood.

"Make a picture for us, Horace!" the neighbors said.
And Horace did.

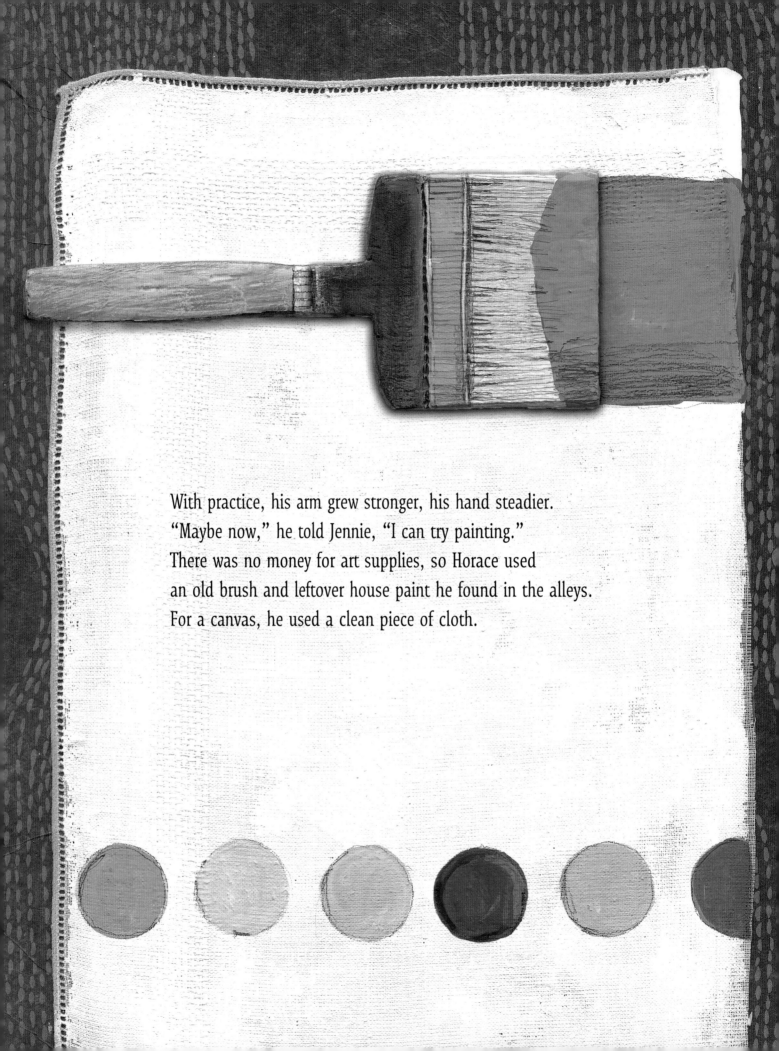

With practice, his arm grew stronger, his hand steadier.
"Maybe now," he told Jennie, "I can try painting."
There was no money for art supplies, so Horace used
an old brush and leftover house paint he found in the alleys.
For a canvas, he used a clean piece of cloth.

Every day, and late into the night, Horace worked on his painting.
He used gray, black, and white, the somber colors of war.
Here and there, he added a splash of red.

If a man knows nothing but hard times, he will paint them, for he must be true to himself...

He used one hundred layers of paint; he decorated the frame
with tiny sculptures. Three years later, he finished.

I go over that picture in my mind several times, and when I am ready to paint it, I have all the details I need.

Now, as he delivered laundry or fished in the river, new ideas came.
But he didn't paint them right away. Before he reached for a brush,
Horace planned each new scene in his head.

He painted the milkman and his wagon, 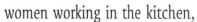 women working in the kitchen,

children playing games in the yard, cotton fields and log cabins, John Brown and Abraham Lincoln,

war scenes and Bible tales, men singing on the corner.

Horace hung his paintings in a shoe-store window.
Five dollars each, said the sign. He hung others in a restaurant.
He even traded one for a haircut. People admired Horace's paintings.
But no one bought them.

Then the president of a local artists' club saw Horace's pictures.
He told his friend, the famous painter N. C. Wyeth, to come see them, too.
Wyeth agreed: Horace's paintings were good. Very good.
"Do you have more?" the men asked.

Horace showed them his work.
He held his breath as they looked and talked.

Finally, they said: "You should have your own art show.
A one-man exhibition, right here in West Chester."
Horace could hardly believe it. He shook hands with the men.
When they left, he celebrated with Jennie.

People came from all around to see Horace's paintings.
Magazines wrote articles. Reporters took photos.
An art dealer told Horace he would help him sell his work.

More than forty years had passed since Horace won his first
box of paints. Now, at last, everyone knew he was an artist.

Horace became famous.
His paintings hung in big-city galleries. Museums displayed them.
Collectors admired them. Movie stars bought them.
Once again, Horace's big hands were always busy.

ARTIST'S SHOW WINS ACCLAIM

LONDON TO SEE PIPPIN PAINTING

Pippin Has Them Talking

A BRUSH WITH GREATNESS

Drawing From The Heart

Does "drawing from the heart" remind you of another artist?

And if you stood outside his house, late at night, you might
see him leaning toward his easel,
his left hand holding up his right,
painting the pictures in his mind.

HORACE PIPPIN was born on George Washington's birthday, February 22, in the year 1888. Though he showed an early talent for making art, he didn't complete his first oil painting until he was more than forty years old. Even after his work was discovered and promoted by such notables as painter and illustrator N. C. Wyeth, critic Christian Brinton, collector Albert Barnes, and art dealer Robert Carlen, Pippin remained true to his own creative process. When someone asked the self-taught artist about his work method, he replied: "I paint it . . . exactly the way I see it."

Fighting in the trenches of World War I proved to be a pivotal experience for the young Pippin. Scenes from those brutal battles haunted him upon his return home, where he was awarded the French Croix de Guerre (Cross of War) and, later, the Purple Heart (for his battle wound) by the United States. He undertook his first adult painting, *The End of the War: Starting Home* (which took him nearly three years to complete), as a kind of physical and psychological therapy. "It brought me back to my old self," he later told a friend. Through daily practice and gritty determination, he gradually regained some of the control he had lost in his injured right arm.

A curious and observant man, Pippin found his subjects almost everywhere. He produced roughly 140 works of art based on childhood memories, family stories, historical reports, photographs, movies, current events, and biblical Scriptures, as well as his own West Chester, Pennsylvania, neighborhood. Pippin's masterful use of color, form, and composition (how the elements of a picture are arranged) is considered his greatest artistic strength.

Today, museums in Philadelphia, New York City, Washington, D.C., Chicago, Baltimore, Minneapolis, Wichita, Buffalo, Charleston, and other cities proudly display the work of Horace Pippin. He has been variously labeled a folk artist, a self-taught artist, and a primitive painter—but he is certainly and indisputably an American master.

AUTHOR'S NOTE

I saw my first Horace Pippin painting (*Saying Prayers*, 1943, oil on canvas) at the Brandywine River Museum in Chadds Ford, Pennsylvania, where I was doing research for my young adult novel *Pieces of Georgia*. The novel incorporates the work of the Wyeth family of artists, including N. C. Wyeth, who first saw Pippin's painting in a store window in 1937 and helped bring him to the attention of the larger world. The rest, as they say, is history. Intrigued by Pippin's unique and powerful style, his connection to N. C. Wyeth, and the fact that he had made his home, as I have, in Chester County, I vowed to learn more about him.

Over the next few years, I visited other museums where Pippin's work was displayed. I read books on his life, catalogs from his exhibits, news articles, and reviews of his work. I visited his house on West Gay Street in West Chester, just a few blocks from where I taught literature classes at the university. Later, once the story was written, Melissa and I retraced many of these paths and forged some new ones. We were inspired and amazed by the very real struggles in Horace Pippin's life and the incredible, simple elegance of his work. Through his art, he transcended personal loss, injury, poverty, violence, and racism, producing a body of work that remains wholly original and deeply American.

Not long ago, I wandered again through the Chester Grove Annex Cemetery, just north of West Chester, until I came upon the granite stone inscribed *Horace Pippin, 1888–1946*. Two small American flags, one on each end, flapped in the wind. The day was cold, damp, and gray—the kind of day Horace had so often described in his World War I notebooks. A mulberry bush arched protectively over the artist's grave, and as I stood there, a male cardinal appeared in the branches, the only bright splash of red in an otherwise dull landscape. Horace, I thought, would have liked that.

—J.B.

ILLUSTRATOR'S NOTE

Typically, authors and illustrators stay fairly separate when making a picture book, but after Jen wrote this text, we bucked the tide by researching Horace Pippin together. Driving through the back roads of eastern Pennsylvania, we shared what we both knew and loved about art and Pippin. His story came to life as we talked to curators who knew his work, looked at Pippin's paintings and his burnt-wood panels, and visited his home in West Chester.

The illustrations for this book were rendered in watercolor, gouache, and collage, inspired by Pippin's deep, rich colors. When it came time to illustrate the art supplies he won in the contest, I knew the actual ones were long gone. But I was so struck by that moment—it brought back all the excitement I felt as a child with a new box of crayons, a ream of construction paper, or a tin of colored pencils lined up in consecutive hues. I re-created the brushes and pencils, which I carved from basswood and painted to look as realistic as the ones Horace might have received. I learned, too, that once he got those art supplies, Pippin used them to make small oval paintings on muslin of Bible scenes. I've imagined one of those paintings on the title page.

One of the things I love about Pippin's art is how he limned his subject matter, making it all the more brilliant. But it was not only Pippin's paintings that inspired me—it was his words. Lettering Pippin's quotes within the illustrations gave me a way to illuminate his simple and heartfelt approach to making art.

I am grateful for the chance to look long and hard at Pippin's life and work. And I'm sure I will never use the color red in quite the same way again.

—M.S.

FOR FURTHER READING

Horace Pippin. Introduction by Romare Bearden. Exhibit catalog. Washington, DC: Phillips Collection; New York: Terry Dintenfass Gallery; Chadds Ford, PA: Brandywine River Museum, 1977.

**Lyons, Mary E. *Starting Home: The Story of Horace Pippin, Painter.* New York: Charles Scribner, 1993.

Rodman, Selden, and Carole Cleaver. *Horace Pippin: The Artist as a Black American.* Garden City, NY: Doubleday & Co., 1972.

Stein, Judith E. *I Tell My Heart: The Art of Horace Pippin.* Philadelphia: Pennsylvania Academy of the Fine Arts with Universe Publishing, 1993.

3 Self-Taught Pennsylvania Artists: Hicks, Kane, Pippin. Pittsburgh: Carnegie Museum of Art, 1966.

**Venezia, Mike. *Horace Pippin.* Getting to Know the World's Greatest Artists series. New York: Children's Press, 2008.

Wattenmaker, Richard J. *American Paintings and Works on Paper in the Barnes Foundation.* Introduction by Derek Gillman. Merion, PA: Barnes Foundation, 2010.

Wilson, Sarah J., and Ann Barton Brown. *Horace Pippin: A Chester County Artist.* West Chester, PA: Chester County Historical Society, 1988.

**For young readers

FILM

Freeman, Linda. *Horace Pippin: There Will Be Peace.* Chappaqua, NY: L&S Video, 1996.

WEBSITES

aaa.si.edu/collectionsonline/pipphora • Horace's notebooks and letters. Details of World War I days and correspondence with his art dealer, Robert Carlen.

archives.gov/education/lessons/369th-infantry • Details and photographs of the 369th Infantry Regiment, of which Horace was a member.

barnesfoundation.org/education/educators/art-of-looking-pippin • "The Art of Looking" project uses Horace's *Giving Thanks* as a teaching tool.

www.brandywinemuseum.org/audiotours.html • Audio introduction to *Saying Prayers* and brief biographical narration.

explorepahistory.com/hmarker.php?markerId=1-A-1A0 • Location and description of Horace's home in West Chester, Pennsylvania, where he created his paintings.

explorepahistory.com/search.php?keywords=horace+pippin&category=2 • Image gallery showing selected works by Horace.

philamuseum.org/collections/permanent/46280.html?mulR=22968 • Enlarged image and audio introduction to Horace's first painting, *The End of the War: Starting Home.*

ACKNOWLEDGMENTS

For their artistic and historical expertise, the author and illustrator wish to thank the following:

Jane Flitner, associate educator, and Christine Podmaniczky, associate curator, N. C. Wyeth Collections, Brandywine River Museum; Pam Powell, photo archivist, Chester County Historical Society; Cheryl Leibold, archivist, Gale Rawson, museum registrar, and Tony D'Antonio, volunteer, Pennsylvania Academy of the Fine Arts; Diane Geis and Carol Welch, reference librarians, Chester County Library, Exton, Pennsylvania; and Ashley Carey, department assistant, Philadelphia Museum of Art.

QUOTATION SOURCES

"The colors are simple, such as brown, amber, yellow, black, white and green." "I go over that picture in my mind several times, and when I am ready to paint it, I have all the details I need." • Pippin, Horace. "How I Paint." *Masters of Popular Painting: Modern Primitives of Europe and America,* exh. cat., pp. 125–126. New York: Museum of Modern Art, 1938.

"Pictures just come to my mind . . . and I tell my heart to go ahead." • Richardson, E. P. *Painting in America: The Story of 450 Years,* p. 389. New York: Thomas Y. Crowell Co., 1956. As quoted in *I Tell My Heart: The Art of Horace Pippin,* by Judith E. Stein, p. 48. Philadelphia: Pennsylvania Academy of the Fine Arts with Universe Publishing, 1993.

"The good old U.S.A. was in trouble with Germany." • Pippin, Horace. "My Life's Story." *3 Self-Taught Pennsylvania Artists: Hicks, Kane, Pippin,* exh. cat. Pittsburgh: Carnegie Museum of Art, 1966 [u.p.].

"I have not seen the sun in more than a month." "The war brought out all the art in me." "I can never forget suffering and I will never forget sunset. I came home with all of it in my mind." • Horace Pippin notebooks and letters, circa 1920, 1943, Archives of American Art, Smithsonian Institution, Washington, DC.

"If a man knows nothing but hard times, he will paint them, for he must be true to himself." • Rodman, Selden. *Horace Pippin: A Negro Painter in America,* p. 5. New York: The Quadrangle Press, 1947.

"It is some of the purest expression I have seen in a long time." • N. C. Wyeth quoted by unknown reviewer in "Horace Pippin Is Called a 'Discovery' at Exhibition," June 1937. Robert Carlen Gallery Papers, Archives of American Art, Smithsonian Institution, Washington, DC.

"I paint it . . . exactly the way I see it." • Edward Loper, interview with Marina Pacini, May 12, 1989, pp. 34–35. Archives of American Art, Smithsonian Institution, Washington, DC.

"It brought me back to my old self." • Theodore Sandford. "Call Pippin Greater than Tanner." *Baltimore Afro-American,* May 13, 1944.

CALIFORNIA

SAN FRANCISCO

LOS ANGELES

MINNESOTA

MINNEAPOLIS

CHICAGO FORT WAYNE OBERLIN YOUNGSTOWN

ILLINOIS INDIANA COLUMB

CINCINNATI OHIO

KANSAS WICHITA

TEXAS

HOUSTON

1941: *SELF PORTRAIT, 1941*
ALBRIGHT-KNOX ART GALLERY
BUFFALO, NEW YORK

⭐ PLACES WHERE
YOU CAN SEE
HORACE PIPPIN'S
ART

1930: *THE BEAR HUNT I*
CHESTER COUNTY HISTORICAL SOCIETY
WEST CHESTER, PENNSYLVANIA

1935: *CABIN IN THE COTTON I*
THE ART INSTITUTE OF CHICAGO
CHICAGO, ILLINOIS

1930: *THE END OF THE WAR: STARTING HOME*
PHILADELPHIA MUSEUM OF ART
PHILADELPHIA, PENNSYLVANIA